In the Beginning

IN THE BEGINNING

Myths of The Western World
retold in poetry and prose

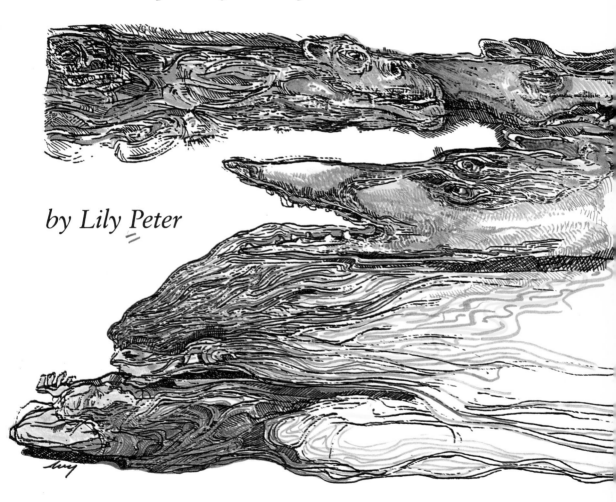

by Lily Peter

illustrated by Ralph Ivy

The University of Arkansas Press

Fayetteville, 1983

The communicating creatures—human and otherwise—on
the title page suggest the dreamlike nature of myths that
will haunt us forever, often frightening, often all magic and
mercurial, often confusing the animal and human worlds (our
animal and human natures), but always and finally coming
through to us in their most human and captivating forms out
of our dreams, our distant past, our suspicions and mysteries
and worshipful confusions, our deep and endless awe.

The publication of this book was funded in part by
The Arkansas Endowment for the Humanities.

Library of Congress Cataloging in Publication Data
Peter, Lily.
   In the beginning.
   1. Mythology—Poetry.   I. Title.
PS3566.E75I5   1983   811'.54   82–20274
ISBN 0-938626-15-9
ISBN 0-938626-18-3 (pbk.)

Contents

Prefatory Note

In the Beginning is a very small book on themes so far-ranging that many books would be required to do them justice. From each of the five great myths of the Western World I have chosen a single episode, incident, or concept that I thought worthy of serious consideration in our modern life, which I have presented as briefly as possible and as nearly as possible in the context of the people whose myth was represented. From the Egyptian myth I chose the funerary ritual of the *Book of the Dead,* which the Egyptians themselves called the *Book of Manifestation of Life,* in order to present the intuitive thesis of the Egyptian priesthood of five thousand years ago that the Universe is self-created, that God is self-created, that the Universe and God are one and the same. From Greek myth I took the conflict between the sexes, which is continuing today even more violently than it was waged in Greece. From Roman myth I took the concept of world conquest, which is turning up again as an obsession in our own day. From Norse myth I took the incident of Ragnarok, which will be our ending if the nuclear contest is continued. From Celtic myth I took their feeling for the magic and mystery of the Universe, a concept that we need to enrich our own lives.

Since each of the world's great myths first appeared in the form of poetry, this form has been used for the statement of the episode, incident, or concept taken from the myth. The Program Notes on the Five Antiphons are in prose, as being more suitable for this purpose.

L.P.
November 1982

In the Beginning

Prologue

Myth is the antiphon of poet and seer,
orchestrated by Everyman in the culture
and age of its origin:
an achievement more worthy
of study than many a muddled page in his history.

The Bone sings to the Psyche of its memories, drawn
from the depths of instinctive feeling that lie deeper
than Reason, than Logic,
deeper than the holdings of knowledge.
The Psyche responds with its memories, rational, irrational,
and the Myth is born of the Bone and the dreaming Psyche.

Here, through the prisms of human thought and experience,
the ordained forces of Nature appear in harmonic
sequences of anthropomorphic symbols.
Here, the Psyche's intuitive responses to life,
its irrational fears, desires, ideals take form
in personifications, narrations, stringent with meaning,
plangent with the hidden power of subliminal truth:
the provenance of the concept of divinity,
the expression of the magic and mystery of the Universe.
The flow of the Myth, its form, its depth,
is the measure
of the reach of the spirit of man in his moments of dream,
and the angle and direction of his civilization
are determined by the tectonics of his Myth.

I

Egyptian

On the banks of the Nile,
millennia past, the priests
of Egypt,
its poets and men of wisdom rendered
their antiphons in the eternal silence of carven
stone, or gave them to the river papyrus,
the stone and papyrus to go on a dead man's journey,
The Book of the Dead,
so called by grave robbers who found
a copy with every mummy, to guide his journey
to the Judgment Hall of Osiris and life everlasting:
the theme of the Book, "The Manifestation of Life":
life eternal, for those who were counted worthy.

The Falcon of Edfu, that magnificent sculpture,
is the symbol of the spirit of man,
conceived as eternal,
in a Universe eternal:
a theme restated in endless
avenues of concepts recorded on pyramid, obelisk,
hypogeum,
the Valley Tombs of the Kings,
the gigantic ruins of the stone forest of Karnak.

Through the enchanted caverns of *The Book of the Dead,*
with their unearthly shining,
millions of years
reach out their hands in a shimmering vision of Eternity.
Amen-Re, the One God,
the Only One,
Creator of the Universe, Maker of the lesser gods,

the divine forces that do his will in the
Universe,
the Sun his symbol as the maker of life.

The Moon-god, Thoth,
lord of wisdom and intelligence,
the ibis-headed Measurer of Time:
scribe
of the gods,
Keeper of the Word in its sacred
attributes:
Osiris, Isis, and Horus, the divine
family
of Father, Mother, and Son,
the Triad of Redemption:
Hathor, goddess of love and joy,
sovereign
of the dance,
mistress of music and song and the
weaving of garlands:
with Nut, the Sky-goddess, cherishing
the dead
as well as the living:
as the Lady of the Sycamore Tree,
hiding in its foliage at the edge of the
desert, to bring
to the newly dead, the bread and
the water of life.

No people have loved life better than
the ancient Egyptians!
So much did they love it that death,
for them, became
a mirror-image of life,
to be celebrated
with a gorgeous funerary ritual and liturgy

Death, for them, became a mirror-image of life.

dramatic in the extreme, in accordance with the Soul's
entrance into life with the gods.

The mummy of the deceased upon the bier:
the priestly hierarchy robed in fresh white linen,
with incense, sprinklings, libations of oil of cedar:
the fourfold repetition of sacred words:
prayers—in *The Book of the Dead* are the oldest prayers
in the world, unchanged through four millennia:
adorations:
chantings:
ceremonial offerings
of fruits, flowers, wine:
hymns to the gods:
all were symbolic ceremonies to confirm
the deceased in his new treasure of eternal life,
the use of all of his natural faculties therein,
with additional powers to place him among the gods.
A tumultuous processional,
with the wailing of all the mourners,
the weeping of the bereaved,
the lowing of cattle:
as goddess of the dead, Hathor must be remembered
in the form of a cow, to furnish the food and drink
the deceased would need on entering his new life:
but all stately and formal as a court pageant,
patterned and picturesque as a grand opera,
and as irrational.

Do not discount the element
of irrationality, a *sine qua non* of life!
The Psyche delights in dwelling in irrational spaces
and stubbornly refuses to be dislodged therefrom.

The dead man's journey is one of drama and danger.
The Soul of the deceased must cross a terrifying country
between the Land of the Living and the Kingdom of the Dead,

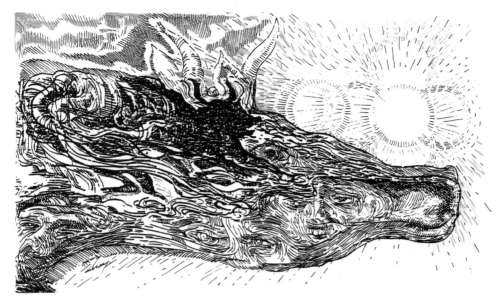

Hathor as goddess of the dead must be remembered in the form of
a cow . . . patterned and picturesque as a grand opera and as irrational.

a realm of demons and darkness,
lakes of fire;
and the one who wanders there unprovided with the knowledge
of the prayers and the magic words that must be spoken
is doomed to the fire-pits of Set,
the god of Evil.

Having crossed this inferno of fiends and flame, the Soul
comes to the borders of the Tuat, the Other World,
a vague, indeterminate region of Twelve Divisions,
wherein are the Great Circles of the dwellings of the gods:
the Ten Mansions of Osiris:
the Twenty-one Pylons
guarding the Tuat,
each with its Gatekeepers, Watchers,
Heralds, Wardens.
Here the deceased must render

The soul comes to the borders of the Tuat.

obeisance to each of these minor deities, giving
the petitions and passwords written in *The Book of the Dead.*

He is ushered into the Judgment Hall of the gods,
the Hall of the Two Truths,
where the Great Nine Gods,
the Little Nine Gods and forty-two Judges await him,
the Judges representing the Forty-two nomes of Egypt.
Here the first Ordeal of Truth is required,
as the Soul makes the Fourfold Confession to each of the Judges:
that he was ever a speaker of truth in all things,
that he had harmed no one by word or deed,
that he had observed strict honesty in dealing
with the property of others,
that he had committed no sin
against the gods or against that which is holy.

The Second Ordeal of Truth
is presided over by Thoth.
In the center of the Hall
is a vast Balance, with the goddess of Justice, Maat,
the spirit of World Order, standing beside it.
Meskhent, goddess of birth,
Renenet, the nurse-goddess,
and Shai, the stern personification of Fate,
taking no notice of the Soul's protestations of innocence,
testify before the gods as to the character
of the Soul of the deceased,
present in the form of a falcon with a man's head,
Thoth recording the statements on his scribe's palette.

In one of the pans of the Balance, Anubis or Horus
lays the figure of Maat,
or her symbol, the Feather
of Truth,
placing in the other pan the Heart of the deceased.
If the Heart is innocent, it is equal in weight to Truth.

Judges await him.

10

The Judges representing the forty-two nomes of Egypt.

Thoth verifies the verdict on his tablets,
and if Heart and Feather are equal, the Nine Great Gods
ratify the favorable verdict,
declaring the Soul's
innocence is proved, and he will not be thrown to Amemait,
the Devourer, the Breaker of Bones, the Eater of Blood,
the Swallower of Shadows,
a monster with the head of a crocodile,
the body of a lion, the rump of a hippopotamus,
that stands by with slavering jaws, to destroy the unworthy.

Then the goddess Maat attires the Soul
of the newly beatified with feathers, the symbol
of righteousness, and he is brought by Horus
to receive the blessing of Osiris:
to dwell forever
in the Fields of Ialu, Amenti, the Fields of Peace.

Five thousand years of antiphon are not to be stated
in a fractional summary.
These are only a few
of the echoes of its forgotten orchestration.
The carven stone yields up its themes in cryptic
and oblique symbols,
and the slender papyrus
speaks in the evening wind with so faint a whisper,
that only the falling darkness makes less sound.

But the thunderous music of *The Book of the Dead*
goes echoing through the streets of the City of God.
"Out of Egypt have I called my Son!"
cries the Evangelist in recognition.
The visions of the Apocalypse are the hybrid flowering
of this frail papyrus, without which Dante could never
have walked with Virgil on the slopes of Hell,
or Beatrice have attained the Paradise of Perfect Light.

II

Greek

The Greek antiphons are as brilliant as spring sunlight
on the green meadows of Thessaly:
all-embracing
as the mountains the Achaeans came through on their journey
    thither:
as vividly human as the willful, imperious,
high-minded poets who formed them in the tragic modes
of the passionate drama and conflict that were the dynamic
warp and woof of their daily existence.

How else could Homer have taken for his epic the sordid
and trifling incident Herodotus records later
in giving the background of the tale of Troy!
Here is the sardonic comment made by Herodotus:
"Certainly the carrying off of women
is the work of a rogue:

Dynasties of gods . . . and demigods.

but to make an ado about such as are carried off
is the mark of a fool!"
This sleazy
scrap of the fabric of living is Homer's theme,
transmuted, transformed, transfigured to the luminous magic
of antiphon,
wrought in counterpoint, fugue, so magnificent
it stands untouched by the wear and tear of millennia!

And the other antiphons of the Greeks, with their intricate
motifs, their dynasties of gods and heroes,
giants and demigods!
Let us pause to praise
anew the poets who left this legacy of myth
enshrined in song: Hesiod, Aeschylus,
Euripides, Sophocles, Aristophanes
and the lyric poets—names woven into the wind,
stitched forever into the wrappings of Now.

The Greek gods came into Thessaly with the Achaeans,
tall, blond, handsome warrior clans from the North,
from the grassy steppes lying between the tremendous
barriers of the Caucasus and the Carpathian mountains,
with a strongly patriarchal culture that included
their Indo-European pantheon, headed by Zeus,
Dyaus-pitar, the Sky-father, a relentless
autocrat who wielded the thunderbolt and the lightning,
threatening the matriarchate of the Mediterranean,
the cult of the Great Mother whom all worshiped
in the lands of the Bronze Age, under numerous names:
Rhea Cybele, Ashtoreth, Artemis,
Ishtar, Isis, Dindymene, Astarte.

Zeus was mighty and potent, with more than twenty
names, and sons and daughters to fill his pantheon
high on Olympus,
where he took up his abode.

But the Mother Goddess was powerful, too, and refused
to accept the cult of the Shining Sky, Dyaus-pitar,
until the deity would consent to be born in a cave
on the Island of Crete,
a shrine of the Great Mother.

And so it was,
and this is confirmed by Euripides,
that the all-powerful Zeus came from his self-created
majesty on Olympus to be born in a cave—
Arkalochori or Dikte or Psychro,
all claim
the honor—as the son of Kronos and Rhea Cybele,
the Mother Goddess herself, in wailing infancy.
Kronos, the Titan, having betrayed and dethroned
his own father, Uranus, and fearful that his sons
would betray him in turn,
had devoured them as they were born.
And to save this infant son, Rhea had arranged
for a number of Cretan dancers, Kouretes, to dance
and sing at this birth and clash their shields to conceal
the sound of his infant squallings
till the babe could be hurried
off to Lyktos,
where his grandmother, Gaia, the Earth,
hid him in a cave on Goat's Mountain and reared him.

So the Great Mother triumphed in this
event, and again, in another spectacular fashion.
The goddess of wisdom, Athene,
whose statue of ivory
and gold by Phidias would later be honored
in the Parthenon on the Acropolis,
was said to have sprung
full-grown from the head of Zeus.
But before this could happen

Kronos, the Titan . . . fearful that his sons would
betray him . . . devoured them.

Zeus had to swallow the pregnant Metis, his first wife,
and Metis is the symbol of Crete, the Great Mother's shrine.
So the Great Mother lived on in a reincarnation
as the immortal Pallas Athene, a non-Greek
name:
the title, Pallas, from the name of the giant
slain by Athene on the field of the Giantomachia,
the war between the ancient deities of Greece
and the Indo-European newcomers, led by Zeus.

The imperial Athene came to be preeminent
in the pantheon on Olympus:
The glorious Parthenon
built in her honor, as the virgin goddess, Parthenos:
her other titles, Alea, goddess of light:
Hygieia, goddess of health: Arcia, of war:
Hippia, tamer of the horse: Chalcinitis, the bridler:
Chalcioecus of the Brazen House, worshiped in Sparta:
Apaturia, for the Ionian festival of the legitimacy of birth:
Nike, as the winged goddess of victory:
Ergane, patroness of the arts: Poliuchus,
the incarnation of law and civic virtue.

In a contest of creative power, Athene
vied with Poseidon for supremacy: some
said Poseidon created a horse: others,
a salt spring.
Athene created in the Erechtheum
the olive tree, said to be the greater boon.

Hera, the consort of Zeus, not to be outdone,
also took over the functions of the Great Mother,
being worshiped as Teleia, the married goddess,
Eileithyia, goddess of childbirth, Chera, the widowed.
The hardest working member of the Greek pantheon

Hecate presided over the meeting place of roads, witchcraft, and magic.

seems to have been Hecate, goddess of the Moon,
the Earth and the Underworld.
Hecate presided
over hunting, athletics, war, the fostering of herds,
the care of children, the meeting places of roads,
witchcraft and magic.

This vast scope of authority
was handed over to Hecate by Zeus himself,
who called her to Olympus,
doubtless glad to be rid

of so many tedious chores of administration.
With duties on Olympus ranging
from the supervision of nurseries to road supervision,
from the Olympian Games to the herding of sheep and goats,
from the Calydonian Boar Hunt to the rituals of witchcraft,
along with the logistics of Peloponnesian warfare,
the triad of heads allotted to Hecate by myth
she needed and could have used more had they been available,
considering the variety and complexity of the undertakings
she was expected to cope with.

Zeus indeed
was probably the first executive in history
to have so talented and capable an office manager,
and a goddess, at that!
But so dangerously
volatile of temper and evil of disposition,
she was always regarded by the Greeks with awe and terror.
Hecate, finally wearying of her multitudinous
duties, resigned them to other gods and became
the incarnation of dark and inscrutable magic.

Aphrodite, the daughter of Zeus and Dione,
his Earth-goddess consort who dwelt at Dodona,
the sea-borne
beauty whom all men yearn for, is the Greek counterpart
of Hathor,
and is also an incarnation of the Great Mother.

Always in the background are the Three Fates:
Clotho,
Lachesis, Atropos, plying their country bobbins,
weaving our lives into patterns beyond our ken:
Atropos, with her ponderous shears, cutting
the thread too soon in foredoom and tragedy.

Always in the background are the three fates . . .
weaving our lives into patterns beyond our ken.

And all this stirring brilliance of a thousand facets
quenched in the shadows of Hades at the River Styx,
confronted with an ill-tempered, bandy-legged ferryman,
Charon,
and Cerberus,
the surly, three-headed dog with a serpent's tail,
guarding the grim entrance to the Underworld,
where Pluto, brother of Zeus and Poseidon, reigned;
and the wailing ghost of Achilles still raved for the sunlight
of the regions above,
declaring it was better to be
a swineherd on earth than a king in the realm of the dead.

There was a scene on the shield of Achilles, known
to Homer's warriors and described in the *Iliad,*

"the god depicted a dancing floor like the one that Daedalus designed in the spacious town of Cnossus for Ariadne of the lovely locks. Youths and maidens were dancing on it with their hands on one another's wrists, the girls garlanded and in fine linen, the men in finely woven tunics showing the faint gleam of oil, and with daggers of gold hanging from their silver belts. Here they ran lightly round, circling as smoothly as the wheel of the potter when he sits and spins it with his hands; and there they ran in lines to meet each other. A large crowd stood round enjoying the dance while a minstrel sang divinely to the lyre and two acrobats, keeping time with his music, cart-wheeled in and out among the people."——*Iliad,*
Book XVIII.

This scene is no figment of the imagination,
but a representation of life on the Island of Crete,
a life that the Greeks had seen, had shared and admired,
that seemed to them formed in a pattern of grace
unknown at that time anywhere else in the world.
Remembering this fragment of life displayed on his shield,
and doomed to the twittering ghosts of Homer's Hades,
what could Achilles feel but a bitter agony!

Crete in the ancient days was a verdant land:
a powerful limestone spine rising from the sea,
wooded with fir and cypress, oak and juniper,
fruited with almond trees and mulberry, quince,
with birds in profusion, the picturesque Cretan ibex
leaping on the slopes of its hyacinth-flowered hills,
its civilization
like to no other,
The Minoans were lovers of life
in a feminine pattern, as opposed to the masculine Greeks.
They were ruled by a Queen, instead of a King, who chose
as her consort a young noble—the Young Prince
in the famed mural at Cnossus, standing in his sunlit
garden of lilies and butterflies, the prototype.

Except for the citadel of Cnossus and a few villages,
the Minoans were given to a rural mode of living
and a highly sophisticated art they sent to Egypt
as royal gifts to the Pharaoh, by young emissaries
with vases and bowls of flowers and flagons of wine
to the great woman-Pharaoh, Hat-shep-sut—
one Queen to another—
in the annals of visits recorded by Egyptian artists
on the tombs of viziers and other important personages.

The pastimes of the Minoans were music, the dance,
and the incredible games played by the youths
and maidens with the tamed bulls, gentled from calfhood
to stand like pylons while the reed-slim girls and young men
sailed through the air like birds, to alight on their horns.

The Greeks loved Crete, and loving its loveliness,
they made its life the dream of their own in Elysium,
the flower-strewn Elysian Fields that were placed by Homer
on the Western Edge of the World:
by Hesiod and Pindar,
an asphodel joy in the Isles of the Western Ocean.

III

Roman

At the head of the Roman Pantheon was Jupiter,
whose name came from the same Indo-European
myth that provided Zeus for the Greeks—the Sky-father,
originally the Light-bringer of prehistory,
to the primitive peoples in the lands where the Sun was worshiped.
The dominant triad of the earliest Romans was composed
of Jupiter, Mars, at that time protector of the fields,
and Quirinis, god of war.
Later, Quirinis
was identified with Romulus, and Mars
became the invincible war-god of the Romans.

The Romans, obsessed with conquest, where shiftless in myth-
      making,
their antiphons lacking in unity and in substance,
from being adopted myths of the peoples they conquered.
A distinction was made between their gods from Italia

and those who were brought to Rome from foreign lands:
the gods from Italia were called *di indigeter,*
and the foreign gods were called *di novensides.*

The Lares and Penates who were their household gods,
Vesta and the Vestal Virgins, guardians of the hearth,
Ceres, goddess of growing vegetation,
Quirinis, Mars, and Saturn, god of the sowing,
came from the rude tribes along the Tiber,
who had lived on the Seven Hills for centuries
before Romulus, when Italy was called Ausonia,
from Auson, son of Ulysses, their fabled progenitor.
Two-faced Janus, the god of beginnings and endings,
Fortuna, Minerva, and Venus came from the Etruscans,
as did the four Agonia, their religious festivals,
in January for Janus, in March for Mars,
in May for Vediovis, the underworld god of death,
the fourth in December for a deity now forgotten.
Vulcan, armorer of the gods, was brought to Rome
by the king of the Sabines, Titus Tatius.

Of the foreign gods, the cult of Phrygian Cybele
was one of many brought from Asia Minor.
The Great Mother cult of Isis
they brought from Egypt and built for her temples,
one near Rome, dedicated by Caracalla,
another in Rome itself, by the same emperor,
and Isis appears on Vespasian's imperial coinage.
Osiris and Horus, Hathor, Sarapis, the Romans
adopted, and for further sophistication,
and a veneer of prestige, they sent an official
embassy to Athens in 217 B.C.,
to bring back to Rome twelve of the principal deities
of the Greek pantheon,
which were set up as gilded statues
on the arid and blood-soaked soil of the Roman Forum.

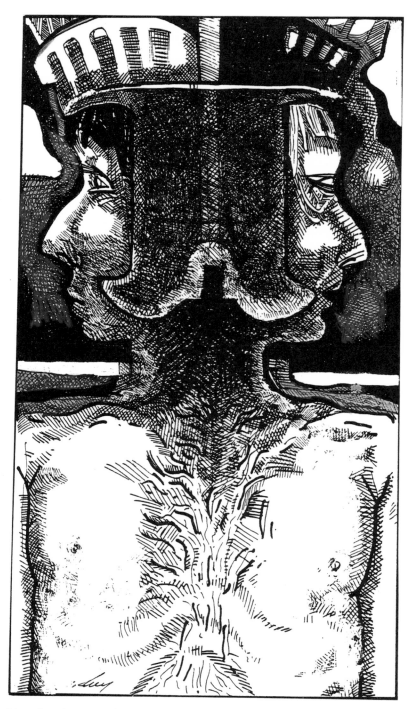

Two-faced Janus, the god of beginnings and endings.

The Romans had an addiction to the concept of empire,
a hydra-headed monster that feeds on blood,
and, like a temple Dagon, must be cosseted
with the paraphernalia of power, to bind it together,
its warped and fragmented entity supported
with the steel of hard-eyed legions,
barricades of law,
to keep it from falling on its face in the midst of the temple,
to the horrified consternation of priest and worshiper.

Empire was their one antiphon, if so this bitter
jangling that echoed from the Pillars of Hercules
to the banks of the Indus,
from the Nile to the Thames, might be called.
And they worshiped at its shrine in Rome,
the temple of Janus,
whose doors were seldom closed,
and in all lands they came to,
with a paranoid zeal for a decade of centuries,
until shrine and antiphon crashed about them in ruins.

The Roman imagination, starved at the root,
yielded a puny growth,
its anemic quality
showing in the way they named the months of the year.

The peoples of antiquity gave to their months rich
and incantatory names:
the mysterious lunar cycle,
with its waxing and waning, being the gift of the gods,
whom they honored in naming certain of these cycles
for the gods who were nearest their hearts
or for those whom they felt
constrained to propitiate for fortune and felicity.

The Egyptians gave their first honors to Thoth,
god of wisdom, to whom they were devoted.
Their year began with the heliacal rising

of Sothis, the Dog-Star, Sirius, on the first day of Thoth,
and of Aket, autumn, the Season of Inundation,
when the land of Egypt was refreshed and restored by the Nile.
The third month of Aket was given the name of Hathor,
goddess of love and garlands, of music and joy.

The Greeks, whose year began with the summer solstice,

Vulcan, armorer of the gods, was brought to Rome.

named their first month for Hecate,
the demoness office-girl
of Zeus, who, when not looking after the weather,
was likely to be roaming somewhere on his own business,
thinking up ways to transform himself into a cuckoo,
a swan, or a bull, to impress the ladies he met.
Next, after seeking the scanted favors of Hecate,
who looked after most of their daily affairs,
the Attic
Greeks of the Isles and of Athens honored Poseidon,
god of the sea,
rendering him double homage,
in that, when intercalation was needed to balance

the length of the year,
the month that was added was known as Poseidon II.

The Macedonian Greeks,
being inland, ignored Poseidon, but showed their judgment
and tact in a neat solution.
To avoid offending
any of the heavenly deities, the first month
of their year, which began with the autumnal equinox
they named for all of the gods, calling it Dios.

The Romans named the first month of their year,
which began with the greening days of the vernal equinox,
for Mars, as might be expected.
Janus, invoked for victory in battle, was placed
in the calendar along with Maia,
daughter of Mercury,
and consort of Vulcan, the maker of battle array.
In the time of Numa,
remembering their many sins,
the Romans made Februarius their Ash Wednesday
of Atonement.
Since even the stolid Roman was stirred by the springtime
opening of bud and blossom, *aperio,* someone,
a poet, perhaps, found a variant in lovely Aprilis.
June was a hearthside gesture to the queen of the gods;
and to Julius Caesar and Augustus they dealt out permanent
honors, as to the gods,
replacing the ancient
numerals, Quintilis, Sextilis, with the founders of empire.

But having reached this point of improvisation,
they could do no more,
and the last four months of the year
they fobbed off with a dull sequence of numbers,
as they named their sons—Tertius, Quintus, Octavius—
poverty-stricken indeed in their nomenclature.

30

Though happily for us, the words September, October,
November, December,
have a pleasing sound
from the Latin language, which owes its origin
to a background far antedating the fatal antiphon
that ended in desolation and lamentation.
In the Romans' acceptance of the Stoic philosophy,
they went somewhat astray from Zeno's original
concept of the Universe revealing itself
as the embodiment of the divine mind.
Their minds poisoned with a jealousy that would not allow
Carthage to stand as the exotic symbol
of a culture differing from their own, they made
the luminous concept of Zeno into a tight-lipped
emphasis on things material that matched their myth.

Zeno's vision in seeing the world as the work
of divine wisdom, governed by laws that men
should study to observe, was distorted into a stern
repression of life's creative, intuitive values,
joy and sorrow alike being interdicted.
The penalty
for this is known, and the Romans paid it.

The other
philosophy of the time that attracted the Romans,
the Epicurean,
was misunderstood as completely.
The Roman mind, bounded by two errors,
on the one hand, a quasi-asceticism, on the other, orgy,
found few consolations in their sterile myth,
with the Golden Apples of the Hesperides—
note that the Apples are made of gold,
nourishing
neither man's body nor his spirit—
the myth's ending.

IV

Norse

The Norse myths have the turbulence of Boreas.
For our Nordic forefathers, theirs was a savage land
of tempest and gloom, subarctic ice and snow,
and their antiphons ring like steel on rime-chilled granite.

In the inconceivable cold of the primeval void
The Unknown God Whose Name Is Not Spoken brought
the creative power of heat and fashioned from droplets
of snow a shapeless monster, the frost-giant, Ymir,
and from the ice-cold fog, the Cow Audhumla.

From the stones of the salty frost the Cow Audhumla
licked forth the demigods, Odin, Vili, and Ve,
who killed the monstrous and evil giant, Ymir,
and formed from his blood, the sea:
from his flesh, the Earth:

from his bones, the mountains and rocks:
from his hair, the forests:
from his skull, the sky:
from his brain, the sullen clouds.

This episode symbolizes the world's creation
through the forces set in motion by The Unknown God,
Odin, Vili, and Ve being temporal gods,
demiurgi, typifying Spirit, Will, and Holiness.

Far to the North lay Asgard,
the sky-rimmed citadel
of the demigods, with twelve great Realms, or Mansions,
that could be reached only by the Bridge of the Rainbow.
Here dwelt Odin, king of the demigods; Thor,
ruler of the thunderbolt; Tyr, the god of war;

Thor, ruler of the thunderbolt.

Famous indeed was the jeweled necklace of Freya.

Loki, contriver of discord and mischief-making,
with other gods and goddesses of the pantheon.

The Norse goddess of love and beauty was Freya,
not to be confused with Frey, god of fertility,
or Frigga, goddess of marriage and the hearth.
Frigga was the wife of Odin and the Sky-goddess,
the constellation Orion being her distaff.
She shared with Odin in the governance of the Universe
and the knowledge of its fate, as subject to mortal law
set by The Unknown God Whose Name Is Not Spoken,
who only was eternal and immortal and the source of life.

Freya dwelt at Asgard in one of the twelve
Mansions, Sessrymnir, an ornate and splendid hall,
where she entertained half of the heroes at Valhalla.
Famous indeed was the jeweled necklace of Freya,
which was given to her by the dwarfs and coveted by Loki,
who tried to steal it but was foiled by Heimdallr,
Warder of Asgard,
who could see a hundred leagues
in any direction, by day or by night;
who could hear
the grass or the sheep's wool grow,
and whose need for sleep
was less than a bird's.
When the fated hour should come to Ragnarok,
it was Heimdallr who would call the gods together
with his great Giallarhorn, and he and Loki
would kill each other in combat at the end.

Yggdrasil was the great Ash Tree of Existence,
with its three deep roots,
Niflheim, Jotunheim, Asgard,
lying beside the waters of Utherbrunn.
The Three Norn Maidens were the Fates, whose ancestry no one

knows: Urd, the Past; Verdande, the Present;
Skuld, the Future.
Urd and Verdande wove
constantly a web reaching from the East to the West,

Urd and Verdande wove constantly a web . . . that was
constantly torn to pieces by Skuld.

from the Dawn to the Sunset,
a glowing and radiant weaving
that was constantly torn to pieces by Skuld, the Future.
And the Norns had other duties, nourishing Yggdrasil
by sprinkling its branches daily with the waters of Utherbrunn,
to keep it from decay, until Ragnarok,
the Twilight of the Gods, should come with the final
clashing of Odin's forces with the forces of Evil,
on the Plain of Vigrid, where even the gods must die.

As one of the symbols of myth, we find the Serpent.
Here it is the Dragon Nithogr, gnawing forever
at Niflheim, the first of the three roots of Yggdrasil,
the lowest of the Nine Worlds, hard by Jotunheim,
where lies the bottomless Well of Mimir,
the Fountain of Wisdom.
In the far North,
where the terms of survival were difficult,
the status of the warrior was glorified.
The bravest who fell
in battle were borne to Valhalla by blooming Valkyries,
who served rich food and flagons of honied mead
to the transported heroes who sat at table, feasting
on the flesh of the boar, Sachrimmer, eaten each day,
and at night made whole for the next day's banquet.
In lands
that were three-fourths winter, famine was always in sight,
and the vision of feasting forever was paradise
to these crowing warriors recounting their battle exploits,
as they flung the feast-bones under the table and shouted,
"Wes heill! Wes heill" in rounds of good fellowship.
And so fond were these heroes, *Einherjar,* of combat, that when
they were not eating and drinking, they were hewing at each other.
But for all their rude appetites, these Gothic forbears
consider, in their runes, the secret forces of the universe;

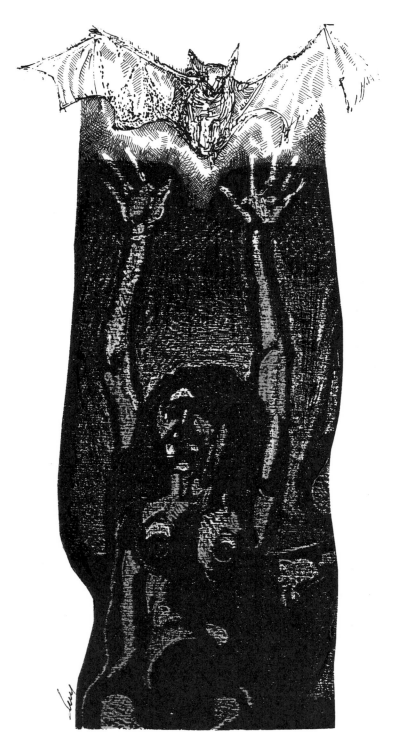

The Twilight of the gods.

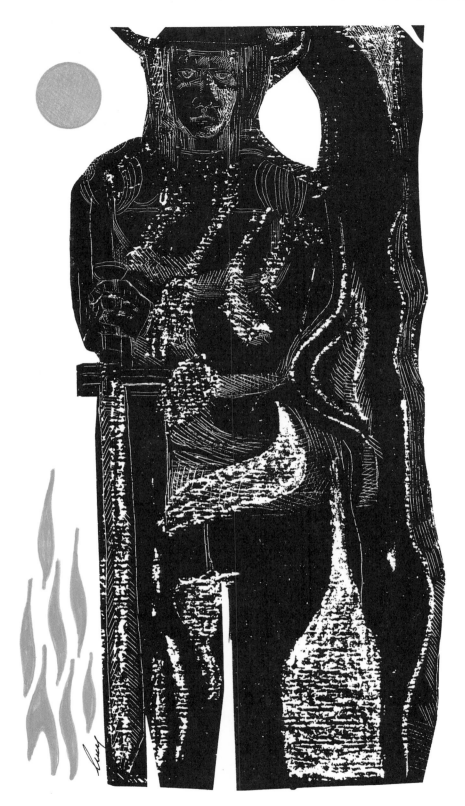

The warrior was glorified.

and in the High Song of Odin, the Lay of Sigdrifa,
their praise is for the virtues of freedom, justice, integrity.

The inexorable Goths intuitively recognized
the Second Law of Thermodynamics a thousand
years before it was put in the records of science.
Each entity bearing in itself the seeds of destruction,
Living and Nonliving come to the same doom,
and the universe renews itself on its own terms,
provided by The Unknown God too great for man's knowledge.

The world and all within it would perish at Ragnarok,
an event preceded by ages of crime and horror,
as the world's antagonisms steadily grew more lethal,
until brother is set against brother, son against father.
The Old Hag of the Ironwood, Angerbodha,
a giantess, mother, by Loki, of the Fenrir-wolf,
the Midgard-serpent and Hel, goddess of the dead,
sits in the East at Midgard, watching her brood
of ravening wolves:
the Fenrir-wolf, that swallows the Sun:
Mannegarm, that devours the Moon, as the stars
are hurled from the high heaven.
The Midgard-serpent,
writhing in giant rage, overwhelms the land.

Yggdrasil, its branches tormented by howling
winds, crashes in ruin.
The Ship of Death, Naglfor,
constructed of the nails of dead men, now floats,
completed, on the world's waters.
He who dies
with his nails unpared furnishes forth the timber
for the building of this bark, dreaded by gods and men.

At the head of the host of gods and the hosts of heaven,
come in their bright armor from Muspelheim,

once the abode of the Sun and Moon and Stars,
Odin rides, dressed as a bridegroom, to battle
with the forces of Evil, knowing it is certain death.
The conflict is terrible, past all telling:
gods
and giants perish:
the earth sinking into the sea:
wild flames engulfing the sky in total destruction.
But The Unknown God Whose Name No Mortal May Speak
provides for the regeneration of the world.
Balder and Hoder, Light and Darkness, return.
Odin's two sons, Vidar and Vale, return
as the forces that make the earth a habitation.
Thor's two sons, Mode, who is Courage, and Magne,
Strength, come back to rebuild the wide Wind-home.
And a single pair, Life and Desiring Life,
who survive Ragnarok,
hidden in Hodmimer's forest,
that even the flames of Surth could not destroy,
who are willing to accept as their food the dew of heaven,
begin the new cycle of existence,
repeopling the world.

So much treasure of concept nearly forgotten!
But the Norse antiphons still live in our common speech,
in the days of the week
that echo the names of their demigods:
the Day of the Sun,
the Day of the Moon, Tyr's Day,
the Day of Woden or Odin, Thor's Day, Frigg's Day,
the Day of Saturn or Saetare, gods of the sowing:
arranged with the eloquent logic of symbolism.

Woden, as king of the gods, had the place of honor,
Four being the holy number of perfection.
Aware that Evil lay everywhere next to the Good

the Nordic seers placed Tyr, the god of war,
of human suffering, on one side of Woden;
on the other side, Thor, the god of Nature's travail,
the gale, the thunderstorm, and the deadly lightning.
The Sun and the Moon,
the heavenly sources of life,
were invoked at the week's beginning:
at the week's ending,
the protectors of human love and the sowing of seed.
Even from frailty, Faith reaches for man's continuance.

V

Gaelic

The Celtic myths are almost lost to oblivion
from not having been committed to writing at the time
they were held to be valid by the people who created them.
This was also true of the Gaels, the Celts of Ireland,
and their wealth of poetry, legend, history, myth,
was comprised in an oral tradition that was handed down
from one generation to another by their poets and druids.

Like the myths of the Keltoi who lived on the Continent,
the Gaelic myths had no organized theogony,
no cosmogony, no chief god or goddess
as did the Egyptian, Greek, Roman, and Nordic.
Instead of a pantheon the Gaels had a shadowy group
of beings, borderline mortals, borderline demigods,
known as the Tuatha De Danaan, the Tribes of the Folk
of Danu, the Great Mother, who had come from the North

in clouds of mist, displacing the Firbolg,
a semi-mythical, pre-Celtic race in Ireland,
who had been defeated and driven from the land of Eire
by the Formorians, a tribe of demigods of Evil
and Darkness who dwelt in the Ocean, keeping all Eire
in tribute and fear.
The Firbolg who escaped to Greece
were made slaves.
Those who remained in Eire
were defeated by the Tuatha in the first battle of Moytura
and driven into the islands along the coast,
to Aran, Islay, Machlin, and the Hebrides.
The Tuatha, epigoni of demigods, mingled freely
with other tribes of demigods in their rambling.
They were regarded as beings of superior importance,
or as heroes worthy of deference and honor,
but no temples were built to them,
nor were they worshiped.

At the head of the Tuatha De Danaan was The Dagda,
meaning the Good God, but not in ethical goodness.
He was good at what he did, in the pattern of Zeus.
In his mortal guise, The Dagda was the greatest of the ollavs,
the Master Poets, and was also a famed harpist.
His wife was Boinn, the River-goddess, the Boyne,
but once each year, at Samain, a festival
of Lugh, god of light, The Dagda was wedded
in a ritual marriage to Morighân, Queen of the Demons,
in a ceremony to ensure The Dagda's power over Evil.

The Dagda had three sons, Aengus, Aed and Kermad,
perhaps three names for the one son, Aengus;
and three daughters, all of them named Brigit,
pronounced by the Gaels always with a hard g—
perhaps one daughter with three important functions.
Aengus was the god of youth and love.

44

The eldest
Brigit, called later, Brede, was the goddess of poetry.
Her sisters were the goddess of smith-work
and the goddess of healing.

The Tuatha went forth, as aristocrats did, with a retinue:
three druids, three stewards,
three gillies, three horses, three hounds,
and three musicians, called Music, Sweet, and Sweet-String.
The listings of the Tuatha are much confused.
Characters appear as gods
and again as mortals and there is little distinction.
Names of important prototype deities that appear
in almost all of the world myths are missing.
There is no goddess of love and beauty to match
with Hathor, Aphrodite, Venus, Freya,
though beauty was the first requisite the Gaels desired
for their women,
followed by five other favored attributes,
and in this order:

The Gaels has only one great god, Crom Cruiach, whose gold-covered
image dominated the Plain.

a sweet singing voice, sweet speech,
skill in fine needlework, wisdom, and chastity.
The Cymric Celts in Wales had as their goddess
of love and beauty, the Moon, Arianrhod,
lovely with a silver crescent in her hair
and draperies of misty blue over sandals of silver.

Saint Patrick says that before his coming the Gaels
worshiped idols, and in the ancient records
are accounts of a gold-covered image of a god, Crom Cruaich,
said to have been a sun-god, set up on Magh Sleacht,
the Plain of Adoration, believed to have been
in the Barony of Tullaghan, in the County of Cavan.
The Dinnseanchas calls it, "The King Idol of Erin,
and around it were twelve idols made of stones,
but he was of gold."
An ancient Gaelic poem
in the Book of Leinster declares that it was "a high
idol . . . which was named the Crom Cruaich. . . . the brave Gaels
used to worship it,
and would never ask from it satisfaction
as to their portion of the hard world
without paying it tribute."

And the Gaels revered the Twelve Great Stones around it
as the Moon through the Twelve Months,
a druid symbolism to secure the favor
of the Moon and the Months in their ruling over the Elements:
Earth, Air, Fire, Water, the Sacred Four,
by whom all high and mighty oaths were sworn.
And was not King Laoghaire slain by the Elements
for having broken the oath he had sworn by them?

Scattered through the Gaelic antiphons are echoes
of Greek myth, with its legends, gods, and heroes.
In the slow migrations of the Aryan peoples

And the Gaels revered the Twelve Great Stones that
stood on the Plain with Crom.

crossing the bridge-lands of Asia Minor,
the stepping-stones
of the Cyclades, there may have been tribes of the Keltoi
who tarried in the Greek Isles long enough to listen
to the burgeoning myths of their kinsmen,
and they were intrigued
and mingled these myths with their own in tangled memories.

In the recasting, Apollo becomes Lugh
the long-handed god of light and craftsmanship.
Achilles becomes Cuchulainn,
the perfect hero,
whose elegy lives on in "Londonderry Air,"
Composed centuries ago by an unknown harpist
as the lament of Emir for her lover, Cuchulainn,
it was saved for our modern ears to delight in by a blind
fiddler, the last of his craft in Eire, he claimed,
to remember the ancient melody.
And he played it,
passing the time at Londonderry Fair,
where an English music lover, hearing its haunting
cadences, wrote it down, preserving its loveliness—
a tiny fragment of the centuries of lost music
in a land where all were lovers of sweet singing.

Dainceht, the leech, is the Greek god of health, Paion,
whose name was given to the peony, that charming flower.
Guibniu, the smith, who was skilled in the making of weapons,
was the Greek Hephaestus.
The Gaelic god of the sea,
to match Poseidon, was called Mannanann, Mac Lir,
the Son of Lir, and later known simply as Lir.

In addition to the gods taken from Greek myth,
in the Gaelic antiphons are memories of Vedic deities
in triads from the tradition shared by the Keltoi
with the ancestors of the Hindus, triads intended

A blind fiddler, the last of his craft in Eire, it was said,
to remember the ancient melody.

not as trinitarian, but in the Hindu sense
of three units treated as one:
the three names of the goddess of war, Meadhbh,
Macha, Morighan:
the three daughters of Fiachadh,
Eiriu, Fodhla, Banba, the Three Fair Ones,
all meaning the Land of the Gaels, and Eire
was the name chosen for the hawthorn-flowered Island.

The most important element in Gaelic myth
was their delight in magic:
The supernatural
surrounded them everywhere.
They saw the world
as a maze of magical agencies, to be constrained
to their daily needs, as best they might, through ritual,
sacrifice, votive offerings, and incantations.
A pastoral people, their Nature festivals
were rich in ceremonies to entreat their gods
for favors for kine and swine, for sheep and barley.

The Gaelic year began with the Feast of Samain,
on November First, beginning the night before,
a fearsome night when the entire temporal world
was thought to be overrun with destructive forces
of magic, possibly a psychic response to the waning
year, with its outward decline in creative energies,
which must be restored through ceremony and ritual.
This festival, the most important of the Celtic year
was in honor of Lugh, its purpose being to renew
earthly success and prosperity for the next twelve-month.

Three other feasts were held during the year
for entreating their deities:
the second in importance being Beltine,
on the First of May, when the herds were driven to pasture.

The others were Imbolc, on February First, to induct
the lambing season of their flocks of sheep;
and Lugasnad, on August First, to honor
the Nature goddess, Tailltu, a queen of the Firbolg,
and foster mother of Lugh,
who is said to have founded
this festival in her honor.
The Lugasnad
held at Telltown, in County Meath, has recently
been revived as the Telltown Games, celebrated
around the great mound where Tailltu is said to be buried.

In the rituals and the incantations of magic,
the Gaelic druids had an important part,
but their lore was an oral tradition and with their death
it perished altogether, and never can be recovered.
The druids do not appear to have been connected
with any rites of worship, and still less
do they seem to have functioned as an established priesthood.
They seem to have been regarded as intermediaries
between man and the invisible powers of the Universe.
In the oldest saga-cycles druids appear
as men of the highest rank and related to kings,
and among the Gaels the druid was held in such reverence
the king himself did not speak on a public matter
until his druid had first expressed an opinion.

The Gaelic concept of the life after death
was of a bright Other-World of renewed life,
placed by the Cymric Celts on the sea-washed Island
of Apple Blossoms, Apfellen, Avilion.
By the Gaels it was called Moy Mel in "The Voyage of Bran,"
where the silver and bronze chariots of the sea-god Mannanann,
run over the sea as on a flowering plain;
an island where from trees covered with blossoms,
"the birds call to the hours, in harmony: . . .

unknown is wailing or treachery . . . without sorrow . . .
a fair country, incomparable in its haze . . .
the land from which laughter peals at every season . . .
of lasting weather that showers silver on the land . . .
a beautiful game, most delightful, they play,
sitting at the luxurious wine, men and gentle women,
under a shady tree, without sin, without crime."
And to the brave Mongon, dying, it is promised,
"He will drink a drink from Loch Lo . . .
the white hosts
will take him, under a wheel of clouds,
to the gathering where there is no sorrow."

Who could ask for more than this!

For epilogue, let us turn to the Cymric Celts
for a fragment of one of their antiphons:
Gwydion
was their Sky-god, the Giver of Civilization
and all the arts:
Zeus, Apollo, Prometheus, in one deity:
his name in the Cymric meaning
"The Sayer of Poetry."
And Gwydion was a notable magician:
the meaning of the myth, that only in the magic of poetry
can man come to his own place in the Universe,
where he may say at last, "I am at home!"

Program Notes on the Quintet of Antiphons

For all their diversity in coloring, context, form, and dynamics, the antiphons in this quintet have two points in common. Each represents the farthest reach the collective intuitive mind of the people who created it could fathom in their efforts to find a symbolism expressing their interpretation of the Universe in its relation to man. And in each antiphon, the intuitive pattern of divinity represents the comfort to which man's emotional nature turns in its uneasy loneliness in an alien Universe whose plan and purpose defy his understanding.

It is for this reason that the Great Mother is one of the chief divinities in all of the lands of the more or less static Mediterranean world in the early millenna of its history. On the other hand, by the warrior clans invading Europe during the period of the Great Migrations, a patriarchal deity was regarded as a necessary symbol of protection, leadership, and strength.

No one knows how or when or by whom the world's great myths were created. Egyptian priest, Greek poet and philosopher, Roman empire-builder, Viking pirate, druid interpreter of the world's hidden magic—Everyman might share in the making of the myths of his own land. Reason and dream, desire and logic, all colored by the dominant processes of Nature in the environment of each separate people, the mores and organization of their social group—all of these factors are woven together inextricably, and the myth comes to a life of its own, on its own terms. In this web, the elusive butterfly, Truth, may be caught as in no other, with no harm to the ethereal butterfly, that can live in the web forever, shaming the dull Fact and our stolid Perceptions with its exquisite irrationality.

In each antiphon may be found an intuitive expression of man's most poignant dream—a fulfillment after death of the spirit's longing for a more satisfying existence, and we can see in these five world-myths how each in its own way has presented its collective subconscious longings. The Fields of Peace, the Elysian Fields, the Hesperides with their Golden Apples, Valhalla, the apple-blossomed Valley of Avilion, the showery gardens by the silvery meadows of Lir—all are found in the same region in the mind of man.

Egyptian

The essential grandeur of Egyptian myth can be matched only by the magnificence of Egyptian architecture and art. The oldest of the world's great myths, its origins reaching back into millennia of prehistory and protohistory, its validities accepted over a period of perhaps five thousand years by a people of extraordinary intuitive perception, creative imagination, and intellect, it offers a panorama of symbolism unparalleled in the literature of myth.

In the prehistoric period of the Nubian hunter of the Stone Age, the first Egyptian myths seem to have been animal cults, the worshiping of animals having mysterious attributes to which man could not attain—the hawk and the falcon for their power of flight, the cat for its gift of night vision, the ibis for its majesty and grace, to name a few. As the hunter moved into the pastoral period of the Bronze Age, his myths developed also a cattle cult, and the cow, whose milk and flesh would support human life, was venerated, along with the bull, as a symbol of life and virility.

At the beginning of recorded history, in addition to the zoomorphism of animal and cattle cults, there already existed a polytheism of various gods and, side by side with all of these cults, an exalted concept of monotheism expressed in inscriptions on pyramid, tomb, and temple walls in words so magnificently poetic they have not since been excelled. From these texts, dating back to the fourth millennium B.C., it is apparent that from the earliest times the dwellers in the Nile Valley were worshipers of One God, infinite and eternal. Here is an excerpt from these early texts.

"God is one and alone and none other existeth with Him—God is the One who hath made all things—God is a spirit, a hidden spirit, the spirit of spirits, the great spirit of the Egyptians, the divine spirit—God is from the beginning, and He hath been from the beginning. He hath existed from old and was when nothing else had being. He existed when nothing else existed, and what existeth He created after He had come into being. He is the Father of beginnings—God is the eternal One, He is eternal and infinite and endureth forever and aye.—God is hidden and no man knoweth His form. No man hath been able to seek out His likeness; He is hidden to gods and men, and He is a mystery unto His creatures. No man knoweth how to know Him—His name remaineth hidden; His name is a mystery unto His children, His names are innumerable, they are manifold and none knoweth their number—God is truth and he liveth by truth and He feedeth thereon. He is the king of truth and He hath stablished the earth thereupon—God is life and through Him only man liveth. He giveth life to man, he breatheth the breath of life into his nostrils—God is father and mother, the father of fathers and the mother of mothers. He begetteth but was never begotten; He produceth but was never produced; he begat himself and produced himself. He createth, but was never created; He is the maker of His own form and the fashioner of His own body—God Himself is existence, He endureth without increase or diminution, He multiplieth Himself millions of times, and He is manifold in forms and in members—God hath made the universe, and He hath created all that therein is; He is the Creator of what is in this world, and of what was, of what is, and of what shall be. . . .

"God is merciful unto those who reverence Him, and He heareth him that calleth upon Him. God knoweth him that acknowledgeth Him, He rewardeth him that serveth Him, and He protecteth him that followeth Him." *

From a number of passages taken from the texts of all periods it is clear that to the Egyptians the form in which God made himself manifest to man was the Sun, whose earliest name was Ra, later, Amen-Ra or Amon-Ra, and all other gods and goddesses are forms of Ra.

It has been said that the Egyptian myth is a pure monotheism which manifested itself in a symbolic polytheism. The fertile valley of the Nile produced teeming imaginations that continued to create anthropomorphic gods to symbolize the manifold aspects of the Universe and of human life, and the innumerable deities that eventually crowd the Egyptian pantheon through the millennia are the outreach of the restless intuitive mind on all levels to find a symbolism varied enough to account for all of life's manifestations.

It should be noted that the primitive animal and cattle cults of the earliest times persist in the Egyptian pantheon throughout its history, regardless of the intellectual overlay of subsequent millennia. Hathor, goddess of love and beauty, is represented with the horns of a cow. In a wall painting of the Eighteenth Dynasty, Hathor is represented as a cow giving milk to the young Amenhotep II, one of the Pharaohs of that

---

* This passage is quoted by permission from The Egyptian Book of the Dead (the Papyrus of Ani), Egyptian text transliteration and translation by E. A. Wallis Budge. Dover Publications, Inc., New York, pp. xcii–xciii.

famous dynasty of which Tutankhamon was the last representative. Isis, the Great Mother, appears nursing her infant son, Horus, her headdress including the graceful lyre-shaped horns of the addax, an antelope found in Syria and Arabia. Thoth wears the head of an ibis; Osiris, in the great Judgment Hall of the Dead, wears the head of a falcon; Amen-Re, the One God, the Only One, is praised as "the beautiful Bull in the company of the gods" in the same poem where he is honored and venerated for his metaphysical attributes as a universal divinity.

The introduction of this zoomorphism into the art of ancient Egypt was really an outstanding tour de force in art, in the exquisite sensitivity and artistic verity given to it through the skill of the artists who designed and perpetuated it for centuries in their representations of the various deities. How much more impressive is the falcon-headed Osiris, the hawk-headed Horus, the lion-headed Sekmut, goddess of vengeance, the jackal-headed Anubis, god of the dead, the cat goddess Bast, the ibis-headed Thoth, even Thoth as a dog-headed ape—wisdom has many levels and many guises!—than these deities would appear if presented with a merely human visage!

There is no other myth that has in it such a complete symbolic record of man's efforts to identify the outward aspects of the Universe with the infinite cosmic forces of the Universe that we call divinity, as do the myths of ancient Egypt. The Egyptians loved the world around them and they reveled in its manifold beauties. The world, with everything in it, was the work of the One God, the Only One, and they delighted in deifying his creatures, from man himself, down to the scarabaeus, the lowly dung beetle. Man they deified in the person of the Pharaoh, the Son of Ra, and their greatest Queen, Hat-shep-sut, as the Daughter of Ra. In addition to the Pharaohs, during the long history of Egypt two private citizens were accorded divine honors: Imhotep, architect for King Djoser of the Third Dynasty and builder of the First Great Pyramid, known as the Step Pyramid at Sakkara; and Amenhotep, son of Hapu, who was vizier of Amenhotep III of the Eighteenth Dynasty, and who was also a famous architect, a sage renowned for his wisdom, and, we are told, "an initiate of the holy book, Amenhotep had contemplated the beauties of Thoth."

Of the animals deified by the Egyptians, there is space in these comments for only three, the scarabaeus, the crocodile, and the bull. The scarabaeus, a beetle that lays its eggs in dung, on which the young beetles feed, was regarded as the symbol of the resurrection and of everlasting life, and its form was given to the small tablet of stone, or faience, on which the Pharaoh had his scribes incise the royal commemorative edicts or memorials that were occasionally issued.

The crocodile was worshiped as Sebek, a god mentioned in the Pyramid Texts as the son of Neith, the Mother Goddess, said to be the oldest of all of the deities in Egypt who ranked below Ra, and as such she was called on by the other gods to give judgment in the Great Quarrel between Osiris and his brother Set (in early Egypt, the god of darkness, but later, the god of Evil) as to which brother should inherit the throne of Egypt, Osiris being the one chosen. The reason for the extreme antiquity of crocodile worship lay in the fact that at the beginning of history in Egypt these fearsome beasts were in many places so numerous and so prolific they had to be either exterminated or propitiated if the region was desired for human habitation. In some parts of Egypt crocodiles were hunted down and exterminated, but in others, notably the Fayyum, the crocodile was worshiped as a god, his sanctuary at Shedet being known to the Greeks as Crocodilopolis, later, as Arsinoë. Here, in a lake near the temple where his worship was conducted, lived an old crocodile called Petesuchos who was venerated by his devotees to the extent of having gold rings in his ears and gold bracelets riveted on his forelegs.

The worship of the sacred bull, Apis, called by the Greeks Serapis, and of other sacred bulls under various names, dated from the cattle cults of early Egypt, and was still popular when Egypt became a Roman province. The chief center of bull-worship was at Memphis, where Apis was regarded as the incarnation of Ptah, the principal god of that city. Apis lived in a temple near the temple of Ptah, where he was daintily fed and each of his movements came to be regarded by his devotees as an omen of some kind. When the Roman governor of the province, Caesar Germanicus, died in 15 B.C., it was recalled that shortly beforehand Apis had refused to eat some delicacies that Germanicus had brought to him.

The Egyptian myths were never fixed in identity, never subject to doctrine or any rigid formula. Always the myth was embodied in cult, which was subject to constant change and new interpretations. The Egyptian myths, unlike those of the Greeks and Romans, cannot be considered as fixed stories. Their function seems rather to have been to provide a notation of symbols with which to express ideas. If the idea changed, then the symbol had to change. An example of this may be seen in the myth of Osiris, which was one of the oldest in Egypt. This myth underwent many changes, finally coming to the worship of the divine family of Osiris, god of everlasting life, Isis as the Mother Goddess, and Horus, their son. This worship became universally popular during the later dynasties in Egypt, beginning about the Nineteenth Dynasty until after the end of the native rulers, when Egypt became a province of the Roman Empire, the reason for this popularity being that the concept of the divine family held warmth and consolation for the ordinary man, who could identify with Osiris much more readily than with a remote Creator wrapped in incomprehensible clouds of Infinity and Eternity.

In the early myths of polytheism, Osiris is listed in the First Ennead, the Nine Great Gods of Egypt who ranked just below the great cosmic God, Ra, by whatever name he was known at that time. For a further account of Osiris, I quote from Dr. E. A. Wallis Budge, one of the world's most renowned Egyptologists:

"The story of Osiris is nowhere found in a connected form in Egyptian literature, but everywhere, and in texts of all periods, the life, sufferings, death and resurrection of Osiris are accepted as facts universally admitted. . . .

"In course of time we find that the attributes of a certain god in one period are applied to other gods in another; a new god is formed by the fusion of two or more gods; local gods, through the favorable help of political circumstances or the fortunes of war, become almost national gods; and the gods who are the companions of Osiris are endowed by the pious with all of the attributes of the great cosmic gods,—Ra, Ptah, Khnemu, Khepera and the like."

The myth of Osiris is embodied in *The Book of the Dead* is one of noble ideas and rewarding concepts, but Ra is not one of the active participants. It is Osiris who bestows the final blessing of eternal life upon the Soul of the deceased. However, the transcendental presence of Ra can be felt throughout the prayers, hymns, and litanies of the ritual, many of which are addressed to Ra.

The text used in connection with this presentation of Egyptian myth is the *Papyrus of Ani,* now in the British Museum, a copy of *The Book of the Dead* made around 1500 B.C. for Ani, Royal Scribe of Thebes, Overseer of the Granaries of the Lords of Abydos, and Scribe of the Offerings of the Lords of Thebes. It is a full version of the Theban rescension, and although this copy dates from the Eighteenth Dynasty, the text dates from the fourth millennium, and this same text continued to be used in the burial of the dead of Egypt until the end of the mythic period. The title of the book is a misnomer, given to it centuries ago by grave robbers who found with each mummy a roll of papyrus containing these texts. The Egyptian title of the papyrus has been translated as *The Book of the Great Awakening,* or *The Book of the Manifestation of Life.*

It is a remarkable fact that monotheism, with its four basic concepts of God as the Self-created and the Creator of all things, as Existence itself and as the Universe itself, should have remained at the core of Egyptian myth throughout its recorded history. That it did so bears vivid evidence as to its metaphysical validity in human life.

Let us for a moment set ourselves against the background of these ancient concepts. Bounded as we are by birth and death and our fragile mortality, nevertheless we are ourselves self-created by our daily choices. Within our microcosmic bodies of flesh and blood, lie our inner selves, as hidden as Amen or Amon, the myriad manifestations of our Selfhood by whatever name they may be called—the tiny Island Universe of Psyche, Libido, Instinct, Intellect, Ego, Talent, Emotions, Mind, Personality, that each man creates in his own time, unseen while we live. The thought that we are atomic replicas of the Universe that is God may help us to understand that we are His creatures, and in the shining concepts of this ancient myth there may be a new refreshment for some of us who find ourselves in the world four thousand years later but little the wiser.

Greek

The Greek antiphons, realistic and dramatic, moved at a counter-tangent to the metaphysical basis of the Egyptian myth, in placing man at the center of the Universe, on high Olympus in Thessaly, and creating the gods in man's own image. That the Greek gods followed the aristocratic pattern of life portrayed in the *Iliad* and the *Odyssey* is clearly apparent, but this does not keep Zeus from being an irascible autocrat, in a furious quarrel with Hera, throwing Hephaestus, god of fire, out of Olympus for taking his mother's part. Hera, supposed to be the embodiment of stately queenship, has the temper and tongue of the termagant shrew. Mercury, messenger of the gods, is an arrant thief. Zeus is a notably careless lecher, and Apollo, with his youth and handsome looks, is something of a Don Juan. Yet in spite of these all-too-human faults, we forgive the peccadilloes, and the Greek gods and goddesses move through their established realm in the minds of men with a kind of radiant dignity, undiminished in their heroic stature.

The myth of the birth of Athene, in springing full-grown from the head of Zeus after he had swallowed his first wife, Metis, the symbol of Crete, the shrine of the Great Mother, is a crude and violent figure of speech, yet a powerful one, for it states in a dynamic fashion the historical truth that the greatness of Greek civilization was derived from the union of the Great Mother cult of the Minoans of Crete and the patriarchal cults of the Indo-European Achaeans and Mycenaeans who were the early Greeks.

But the union of these two cultures was not easily effected. The Greek women were not the dainty, charming, ultra-feminine type of the Minoans. The Greek women tended to resemble their fathers, in being stubborn, willful, high-tempered, and dominating, and in the conflict of the two myths, irony, ambiguity, ambivalence are present to a surprising degree, along with the irrationalities and contradictions that are common to life and literature.

In their personal relations with their women, the Greeks seem to have had difficulties, which they tried to circumvent. Demosthenes tells us that the Greeks had their women on three levels: pallages, or concubines, for sensual enjoyment; haetira, for intellectual enjoyment; and wives to bear them sons. But this disposition did not work out as expected. The pallages, who were beautiful but dumb, were too stupid. The haetira, who were beautiful and intelligent, were too clever. And their wives nagged them. So the honied arrangement turned to a dull vinegar, and Greek literature, from the earliest times, has a vein of querulous complaining about the ways of women. Hesiod, for one, remarks that the only state worse than marriage is not to be married at all, for then a man would have no sons to inherit his goods or to care for him in his old age.

The ideal of perfect womanhood in Greece was Athene, who became the most powerful personality in the Greek pantheon, and, as such, she represents the highest ideals of the two myths, the two cultures, the Minoan and the Greek. Her numerous titles are indicative of her honors and her renown.

The symbolic myth of the birth of Athene from the head of Zeus has nothing to do with her actual historical background, which is so ancient that no one can trace its beginnings to prehistory. The Egyptian myths are the world's oldest, and we are told that Athene was identified with Neith, the most ancient of the Mother Goddesses of Egypt. We do not know when she came to Crete, but we know from the python that lies coiled and hidden in the shadow of her shield in the Parthenon that for lost centuries Athene was the Snake-goddess of Crete, the protectress of house and palace, and it is thought that her name came from the Minoan.

It is known that the Great Mother of Crete had shrines in Greece during the Mycenaean Period, and it is thought that during the invasions of the barbarians from the North, Athene must have come to Greece as the protectress of the Great Mother shrine that was near the Acropolis when the great rock was fortified with the cyclopean walls built by the Mycenaean kings whose palace was on the north side of the rock near the present Erechtheum. Athene stayed on as the tutelary goddess of the Acropolis, and in time the city was named in her honor.

In our reading of Greek mythology as a whole, it is interesting to note the basic changes in it that took place during the centuries of conflict between the two cultures it represented. As the arbiter of the Indo-European pantheon brought to Mount Olympus by the Achaeans, Zeus took residence as a terrifying autocrat who threw his weight around in much fist-shaking and clashing of thunderbolt and lightning, with the undisguised insolence of a total despot. But as the centuries passed there was a change in the balance of power. In the intellectual life of Greece, in philosophy, poetry, the drama, the arts of sculpture and architecture, the preeminently masculine mind of the great Greeks set standards of immortality that still reign supreme. But in the development of its mythology the more intuitive feminine qualities of thought took over, which made a difference in its final validities. With the preeminence of Athene, Hera, Hecate, Aphrodite, the Three Fates, Clotho, Lachesis, and Atropos, the fearful avenging Eumenides, and, always in the background, Rhea Cybele, the Great Mother, it is evident that in Greek mythology the ladies on Olympus stole the show.

Roman

The antiphons of Rome, borrowed from all of their conquests, with the consequent disadvantage of the nonindigenous, had no deep roots in the life of the Roman populace, who accorded their deities merely a nominal worship, except those having to do with the concept of empire. But out of the antiphon of empire came a strange paradox. The Greek civilization, overwhelmed by Rome, arose from the conquest, like Nike, in victory, and was carried by the conquest to regions far distant, enriching all of the lands of the Mediterranean.

The Roman legions perished with the fall of the empire, but the codes of the Roman law that had held their temple Dagon in place, surviving the chaos that followed the dissolution of the Roman empire, finally became the sinews of a later Europe.

The Stoic philosophy of the period, based upon the premise that all Reality is material, with the grim emphasis on the resigned acceptance of whatever Fate may bring, given to it by the Romans, lent a fitting accompaniment, if a joyless one, to the antiphons of empire. The other philosophy current, the Epicurean, misunderstood by the Romans as one of total license and orgy—the Romans, in general, seem to have been as impervious to Aristotle's Golden Mean as they were to the idealities of Plato—did little to enhance their daily lives. And as to the comfort the Romans may have received from worshiping his bloody gods of conquest and power, with their certain alignments of betrayal and counterbetrayal, the "Et tu, Brute!" of Caesar is the final comment.

The bringing of the Greek gods to Rome was a quaint event that deserves notice, since it is an indication of the state of culture prevailing in Rome in the third century B.C. In the matter of conquest, the Romans were already doing very well, and Rome was being adorned by the loot brought thither by returning legions, but in the matter of culture the nouveau riche Romans were still barbarians. With the spread of Hellenism in the third century, B.C., it had become very fashionable to imitate the Greeks, and in 217 B.C. the Romans sent to Athens an embassy who were commissioned to bring back to Rome twelve of the most important Greek gods. The members of the embassy were so ignorant they did not even know the names of the Greek deities, and they knew only eleven of their own, which they presented in a list, asking the Athenians to match these deities with the Greek deities and to add one more to make twelve, to fulfill their instructions. The charitable Athenians, graciously concealing their amusement, gave to the Roman messengers Zeus to match Jupiter, Hera for Juno, Poseidon for Neptune, Athene for Minerva, Ares for Mars, Aphrodite for Venus, Hephaestus for Vulcan, Hermes for Mercury, Demeter for Ceres, Artimis for Diana, Hestia for Vesta. Since the emissaries could not think of another Roman deity, the good-natured Athenians, knowing that the Romans had no god of music, kindly threw in Apollo for good measure. The gilded statues of these gods were duly set up in the Roman Forum, but we do not hear much about their alter egos thereafter.

From what little we do know, it seems that Zeus, after taking up residence in Rome, became far more circumspect in decorum than he had ever been on Olympus, so much so that he could easily have passed any day of the week as a Roman senator with a mild interest in the weather. Hera, it seems, toned down her tongue and her temper, conforming quickly to the image of the haughty and highborn Roman matron, although no further typing is possible, since Roman matrons varied in ways and means from Cornelia, mother of the Gracchi, to Messalina, mother of Nero, and from Cicero's wife to Augustus's daughter Julia.

However, we have no certain record of the alter egos of these two worthies who were given no choice in their deportation from their home country to an alien land, and it may be that in third century B.C. Rome, Zeus's affairs and Hera's tantrums went totally unnoticed in the many and more violent episodes continually occurring in that city of violence and greed.

It is understood that these comments on the alter egos of the great Greek gods are merely scholarly suppositions that count for no more than a dime a dozen. However, it seems to be a fact that the gods of the human consciousness have, if they are genuine, a life of their own and that this life, like that of the Earth's own fauna and flora, tends to wither when transplanted to an alien environment. It seems that the alter egos of the Greek gods in Rome hardly outlasted the gilding on their Forum-based statues. Aphrodite, that great Lady, who, on occasion, had entertained Anchises, father of Aeneas, fled the crudities of Rome quickly enough, taking refuge in Sicily, where she was welcomed and her cult came to flourish in Eryx.

We can only lament the fact that the vivid and compelling gods of Greece could not enjoy a sea change from their journey across the Mediterranean to the Tiber. Instead, they soon lost their luster and their surging vitality. As heirs of their vibrant actualities in the ancient Greek world, let us continue to enjoy the exponential vigor and the memorable symbolism of their myths that have enriched our literature for centuries past, and to their gilded and faded alter egos in Rome, giving the blessing of a *Requiescant in pace*.

Norse

The Norse antiphons, dark and forbidding in texture as the ocean cliffs of the lands they came from, are markedly different from the other myths of the Western World in the degree of emphasis in their symbolism. In every myth there is awareness of human suffering, wickedness, tragedy, but in most myths there is also a sense of joy, either in the Universe or in human relationships or in both, and somewhere in most myths, a feeling for idealism. Of these elements common to myth, the Norse myth emphasizes mainly the first one mentioned, but even for suffering and tragedy there is little compassion, only grim endurance.

There is an outward splendor in the architecture of Asgard, but the concept of idealism is totally absent in their highest symbol of recognition and honor. Valhalla, in spite of its glorification in grand opera, was for the warriors who gained admittance thereto merely a place of eternal gluttony, varied by contests of physical prowess. And as for the blooming Valkyries who served their menfolk, they seem to have had no better fate than kitchen wenches.

The force of mind inherent in the makers of Norse myth is evident in their superb figures of speech: the Ash Tree of Existence that is Yggdrasil; the Three Norn Maidens; the healing, renewing Waters of Utherbrunn flowing from the bottomless Well of Mimir; the Dragon Nithogr that remains unslain; their intuitive awareness of the Second Law of Thermodynamics; and the crashing annihilation of Ragnarok. The whole myth is dark with no friendly darkness of serenity and peace, but the oppressive darkness of foreboding and danger. Even for Life and Desiring Life, who are willing to undertake the rebuilding of the world following Ragnarok, there is little cheer. The two sons of Thor, Courage and Strength, offer their aid, but to the rebuilders the myth promises only the dew of heaven for their subsistence.

64

As for Ragnarok, that powerful figure of speech that has in it the very sound of doom, we might recall that we ourselves have seen two dress rehearsals of this catastrophe in our own century. Our world is far more fragile, far more vulnerable than was formerly realized. With the arsenals the Titans now possess, a third rehearsal of Ragnarok could be the world's ruin, making the beautiful planet that is the only one we shall ever have a place of lethal deserts, of poisoned oceans for two hundred thousand years to come, which is forever, so far as we are concerned.

Perhaps in this myth of a thousand years ago there is a stern warning for our own day. Our Norse forefathers may have lacked an awareness of some aspects of life that we now consider important, but because they lived in a land where life on any terms was barely possible, they had an acute awareness of danger. We who have lived in relative security all of our lives do not have this awareness. We do not comprehend the danger that we ourselves have created. Ragnarok can be our fate if we do not heed the warning.

Gaelic

The Gaels had a viewpoint unique in history, in regarding poetry as the greatest of all the arts. Their myths, epic tales, history, even their laws, were all in poetry, handed down orally through the generations, and it is a miracle that any of these would have survived. That they did, is due to the quality of the poetry and to the vigor and vitality of the social pattern that sustained it.

The Gaelic bards were in two classes, the Saor and the Daor, the patrician and the plebeian. In each of these there were eight grades, the highest being the *filé,* and the lower grades of bard were little thought of in comparison with him. Where the *filé* received three milch cows for a poem, the bo-bardh (cow bard), the second of the eight grades, might carry away only a calf. For each of the eight classes of bard there were rigid regulations imposed by law and custom as to the meters the poet was permitted to use, and woe be to him who transgressed the rules of the craft by encroaching on the meters of the bard next above him in rank!

The eight classes of the Saor had fanciful names, the fifth, sixth, and seventh being known as the *Tighearn-bhard* (lord bard), the *Struth diaill* (stream from the cliffs?), and the *Anstruth bardh* (great stream of poetry). The designations of the Daor were equally fantastic. After reading and writing were brought to Eire by the monks of the fifth century A.D., bardic schools were developed in which the ancient craft continued to be learned as it was in the old days when it was regulated by oral law and custom. It should be noted that the Sons of Eire took to the skills of reading and writing like starved cats to a saucer of cream, and in no time at all, which is to say, a century or two, comparatively speaking, there were *mac-leighinn,* Sons of Reading, scattered from one end of the Island to the other.

Having reached the rank of *filé,* the aspiring young poet would be faced with the seven grades of *filé* to be completed before he could claim the rank of *ollamh* (ollav). The ollav must have studied from twelve to twenty years to compose in the 350 forms of poetry required by custom. He must be able to recite 250 of the prime epic tales in poetry, many of which pertained to Gaelic myth, and 100 of the secondary tales. He must also be an accomplished harpist, although as court entertainer he always had to be accompanied by a bard, who had to be familiar enough with this extensive body of poetry to be able to follow the chantings of the epic tales with appropriate improvisations on the harp, since there was no such thing as written music.

For the benefit of modern poets, some of whom resent even the simplicities of iamb and trochee, here is an example of one of the meters used in Gaelic poetry. It was called the Deibhide (d'yevvee), meaning "cut in two," and was the generic name of twenty-four species of meter already established in the oldest poetry. In this meter the *aird-rinn,* or rhyme scheme, requires that the rhyming word ending the second line of the poem contain one more syllable than the rhyming word that ends the first line. If in the first line the accent falls on the ultimate syllable, in the second line it falls on the penultimate. If the accent falls on the penultimate syllable in the first line, in the second it falls on the antepenultimate.

There is no known period of history when poetry has been more highly cultivated than it was among the Gaels. In spite of the elaborateness of the system they evolved, the enormous complexity of the rules, and the intricacy and subtlety of their poetic code, poetry in ancient Ireland was so highly thought of and so greatly admired and enjoyed that we are told on unimpeachable authority that the bardic order contained a third of the men of Ireland who were of the free class or patrician, and almost as many in the Daor or plebeian group.

Having no writing, the Gaels had no dramatic poetry, as did the early Greeks, and their poetry is limited to lyric and narrative verse. Ogma, their god of learning, represented the power of speech, which, by its charm, may hold the hearer captive; and since the Gaels have ever been lovers of sweet speech, he was called "Ogma of the Sunny Countenance," and was equated by them with Heracles, who, they claimed, performed his wonders by the power of persuasion, rather than by physical strength and brute force.

In spite of the loss sustained by Gaelic poetry and myth in the transition from an oral tradition to a written tradition, it has had a notable influence on literature, especially the literature of the British Isles, mainly seen in its emphasis on magic, which may be defined as an awareness of and an empathy with the mysteries of the Universe. In our consideration of the enrichment of our literature through this awareness of the magic of the Universe, we should be mindful of our indebtedness to the druids of ancient Ireland, those men whose superior intuitive powers, intellect, and stamina contributed greatly in keeping alive through the dark barbarisms of Western Europe the sense of wonder and of mystery that is the basis of science as it is of poetry and myth. Fragile and few as are these fragments of Gaelic myth, they have provided for us an immense treasure in the timeless magic that shines from them in romance and in legend: *Le Morte d'Arthur,* which includes the legends of Tristram and Iseult, the Holy Grail, many another; the plays of Shakespeare—*The Midsummer Night's Dream, The Tempest, The Winter's Tale*—these are all romances cut from the tapestries of the Celtic imagination. The enchantment of Celtic myth still holds its potency, and Prospero's wand, which was handed down from Merlin, will never lose its magic, though buried for centuries fathoms deep beneath the sod.

We must conclude these program notes with a word about Prospero's wand. Prospero himself was evidently a druid, although it is not so mentioned in the bond. The druid carried with him as the symbol of his high office a wand of yew, and there is a curious reference to this custom in a piece of writing attributed to Cormac mac Art, the most famous king of early Ireland, who lived in the third century A.D. Among his many notable achievements, Cormac is said to have built the first mill in Eire and to have made a banqueting-place of the great Hall of Mi-Cuarts (the circulation of mead) at Tara, which was 100 yards long,

100 feet wide, 45 feet high and was entered by fourteen doors. The site is still to be seen, but no vestige of the building, which, like all other early Irish structures, was entirely of wood.

The writing ascribed to Cormac is by some unknown writer several centuries later, who evidently admired so greatly the achievements of Cormac and his son, Cairbre of the Liffey, that he offers this writing as a tribute to their greatness. We know that the writing is of a later date than Cormac because in it there is a reference to heaven and hell, of which the Gaels had never heard until the coming of the monks in the fifth century A.D. The writing is in the form of a letter addressed by Cormac to his son and was written in prose, one of the rare examples of prose found in Gaelic literature, and the title is *Teagasg riogh,* or "Instruction to a Prince." The letter is in the form of a catechism of question and answer, with the young prince Cairbre being the one who asks the questions of his father. The letter is full of sound wisdom, beautifully stated, and could be read with profit by any young man of the twentieth century, whether or not he is planning to follow the career of a prince.

At one point the young prince asks his father this question: "O grandson of Con, what are the most lasting things in the world?"

To this question the King gives a curious reply: "Grass, copper and yew."

Douglas Hyde, the famous Gaelic scholar, in his *A Literary History of Ireland*, finds this statement "unintelligible." It is indeed a dark saying, but so full of truth the darkness becomes a transcendent blaze. Grass is the symbol of Life itself, which will be here in some form while the world stands. Copper, a nonrusting metal, one of the Hundred-plus Elements, will be here while the Universe stands. And the Wand of Yew, the symbol of mystery and magic, will outlast Infinity and Eternity and all of the Universes that the eons may have in store, in All That Was, All That Is, and All That Is To Come!